Spring is a time of renewal. We rejoice in the signs of new life all around us, and the hope they bring after a long winter.

Fill in the blanks with the missing words. Then write them in the grid where they belong. Hint: Look up the verse in your Bible if you need help: Song of Songs 2:11–12 (NIV).

___ ___ ___! The ___ ___ ___ ___ ___ ___

is ___ ___ ___ ___; the ___ ___ ___ ___ ___

are ___ ___ ___ ___ and ___ ___ ___ ___.

___ ___ ___ ___ ___ ___ ___ appear on the

___ ___ ___ ___ ___; the ___ ___ ___ ___ ___ ___

of ___ ___ ___ ___ ___ ___ ___ has come,

the ___ ___ ___ ___ ___ ___

of ___ ___ ___ ___ is ___ ___ ___ ___ ___

in our ___ ___ ___ ___.

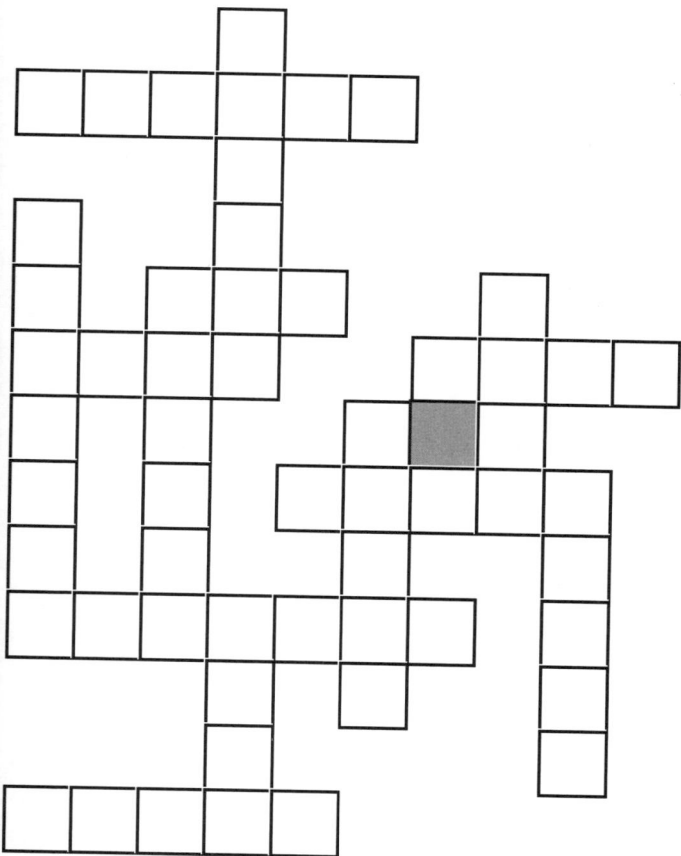

Easter also reminds us of the hope of a new life.
Do you know why this special celebration began?

Use the code to fill in the letters.

I N T H E
14 4 2 21 19

H O P E O F E T E R N A L
21 11 15 19 11 3 19 2 19 8 4 26 25

L I F E , W H I C H G O D ,
25 14 3 19 , 5 21 14 6 21 17 11 12 ,

W H O D O E S N O T L I E ,
5 21 11 12 11 19 13 4 11 2 25 14 19 ,

P R O M I S E D B E F O R E
15 8 11 18 14 13 19 12 9 19 3 11 8 19

T H E B E G I N N I N G
2 21 19 9 19 17 14 4 4 14 4 17

O F T I M E .
11 3 2 14 18 19 .

T I T U S 1:2
2 14 2 24 13

A/26   B/9   C/6   D/12   E/19   F/3   G/17

H/21   I/14   J/23   K/7   L/25   M/18   N/4

O/11   P/15   Q/22   R/8   S/13   T/2   U/24

V/20   W/5   X/16   Y/10   Z/1

4

An amazing event took place long ago. The world was forever changed when God sent His only Son Jesus to earth. We can read all about the life of Jesus in the Bible. Which books of the Bible tell about the life of Jesus?

Shade in every other letter. Write the letters in order on the line below to spell the words. Then use the letters you have not shaded to answer the question. Hint: Some letters will not be used.

T	M	H	A	E	T	F
T	O	H	U	E	R	W
G	M	O	A	S	R	P
K	E	L	L	U	S	K
Q	E	U	J	X	O	N
H	C	N	W	F	D	Y

_____

_____

What do we call these books of the Bible?

___ ___ ___ ___   ___ ___ ___ ___

___ ___ ___ ___ ___ ___ ___ ___

In the very beginning when God created the world, everything was perfect. Adam and Eve and their home, the garden of Eden, were perfect, too. What did God think about His creation?

Write the first letter from the name of each picture on the lines under the puzzle. Do this in number order (1, then 2, then 3, etc.). Then break up the letters into words to read the Bible verse.

__ __ __ __ __ __ __ __ __ __ __

__ __ __ __ __ __ __ __ __ __ .

Genesis 1:9

6

Then Adam and Eve disobeyed God, or sinned. Adam and Eve wanted to do what made *them* happy, not what God asked them to do. Their sin separated them from God.

How did Adam and Eve sin? Go down the first row on the grid. When you come to a shaded box, put that letter on the line below the puzzle. Continue to the end of the puzzle. Then break up the letters into words to read the Bible verse.

A															
D															
E															
F															
G															
I															
K															
L															
N															
O															
R															
T															
V															
W															

They ate from the _____

_____Genesis 2:17

The people God created and loved had turned away from Him to follow their own desires. Poor choices filled their lives with so much pain and heartache.

What punishments did Adam and Eve receive? Write the letter that comes BEFORE the letter under each line to find out.

WITH PAINFUL

LABOR EVE

WOULD HAVE

CHILDREN. WITH

PAINFUL WORK

ADAM WOULD

GROW FOOD FOR

HIS FAMILY.

From Genesis 3:16–19

ABCDEFGHIJKLMNOPQRSTUVWXYZ

God was disappointed that His people chose to sin. God is perfect and holy, and sin cannot be where God is. Adam and Eve had to leave Eden because they chose not to listen to God. Sin separates us from God.

Find the path that will take Adam and Eve out of Eden.

Sometimes we do wrong like Adam and Eve. When people do wrong, they must suffer consequences for their poor choices. What does the Bible say the punishment is for sinners?

Follow the lines from the letters to the blanks they touch. Write the letters to read the Bible verse.

e w S T

a e s h n

s

g o i e t

f

Romans 6:23a

i h a d

Our sin would keep us away from God forever in hell, the place where sinners will be punished. The Bible says,

"When the Son of Man comes...he will sit on his glorious throne. All the nations will be gathered before him, and he will separate the people.... Then the King will say to those on his right, 'Come, you who are blessed by my Father; take your inheritance, the kingdom prepared for you since the creation of the world....' Then he will say to those on his left, 'Depart from me, you who are cursed, into the eternal fire prepared for the devil and his angels'" (Matthew 25:31–41).

Circle the underlined words hidden in the puzzle.

```
E S T H R O N E D L P Y A L V K M V
I E S H E X G L O R I O U S C J H F
A P R W P Z D E P A R T J B R L J V
F A P E O P L E X D F O L Y E R B M
C R A A V O B I N H E R I T A N C E
K A J F A T H E R W R X J Q T D U Z
I T C P K I N G P J O W C A I P R S
N E C T R I G H T U J R D T O O S E
G K G A T H E R E D Q A L R N I E U
D H A I H B J C O M E M M D H I D L
O L I D E V I L D S O N O F M A N G
M W D A P R E P A R E D I P C Y J C
I P B L E S S E D A W L I J L E F T
E T E R N A L F I R E N A T I O N S
```

God does not want anyone to go to hell. He wants us to repent of our sins, so we can be with Him forever in heaven.

What does the Bible say? Use the code to find out.

THE GIFT OF

GOD IS

ETERNAL LIFE

IN CHRIST

JESUS OUR LORD.

ROMANS 6:23b

A=□ C=○ D=☆ E=▭ F=⬡ G=△

H=◎ I=✚ J=◖ L=Ɗ M=☺ N=■

O=● R=★ S=▬ T=⬢ U=▲

12

God knows we will not do the right thing all the time, but He still loves us very much. God longs to bring His people back into a close relationship with Him.

What does the Bible say? Cross out every Q, K, and W. Write the letters you have left on the lines and break them into words to read the verse.

QYOKUWL   _____

ORQKDWA   _____

QKREFWQ   _____

OKRGIWQ   _____

VIKWNGA   _____

QNKDWQG   _____

OQODKAB   _____

WKOUNQD   _____

IKNGINW   _____

LQOKVWE   _____

Psalm 86:5

13

As part of His plan to restore this broken relationship, God sent His only Son into the world.

Write each word of the Bible verse in the grid. A few letters are given to help you get started.

For God so loved the world that he gave his
one and only Son, that whoever believes in him
shall not perish but have eternal life.
John 3:16

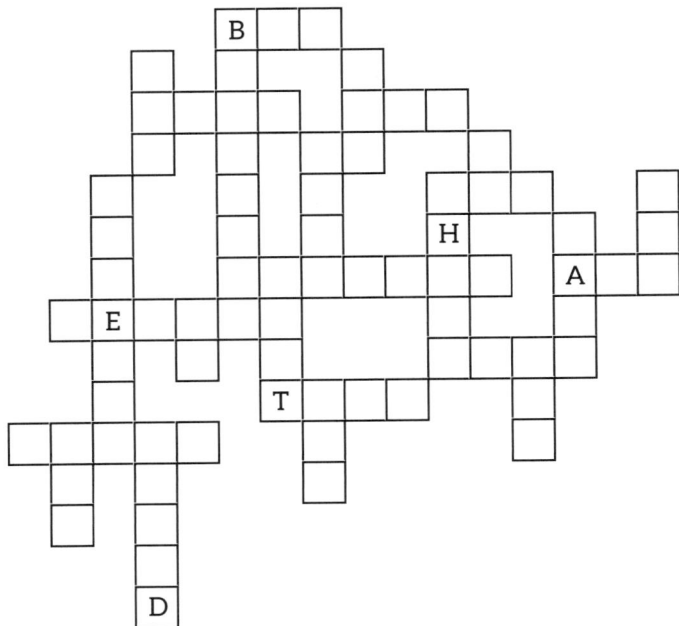

Jesus lived and walked this earth as a man. What does the Bible say?

Use the angle code to write the correct letters on the blanks. Then read the Bible verse.

1:14

A	B	C			N.	O	.P		W
D	E	F	K	L	Q.	R	.S	X	Y
G	H	I		M	T	U	V		Z

He was part of a family, with parents who did not always understand Him. Jesus knew joy and sorrow. He worked hard. He made friends. And yet in an important way, Jesus was not like us. How was Jesus different?

Solve the maze. Then write the words you crossed over in order to finish the Bible verse.

He was _____

_____

_____

_____.

Hebrews 4:15

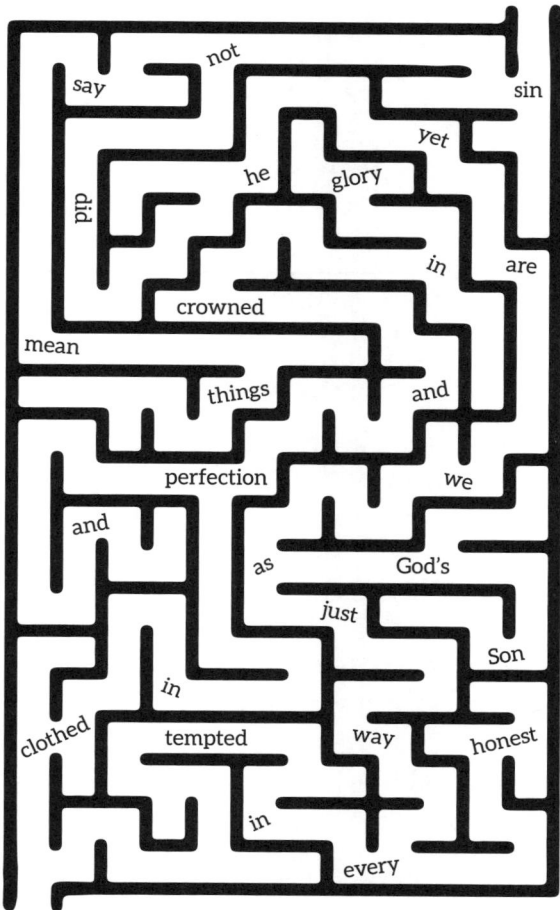

FINISH

say   not   sin
did   he   glory   yet
crowned   in   are
mean   things   and
perfection   we
and   as   God's
just
in   Son
clothed   tempted   way   honest
in
every

START

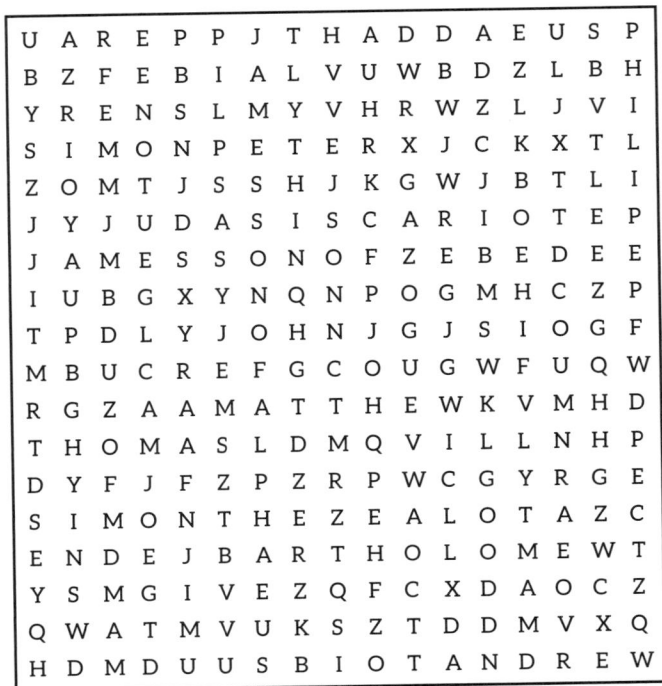

At the age of 30, Jesus began His ministry. He chose 12 men, called disciples, to help with His work.

Circle the names of the disciples hidden in the puzzle.

Simon Peter
Andrew
John
James
(son of Zebedee)

James
(son of Alphaeus)
Matthew
Philip
Bartholomew

Thomas
Thaddaeus
Simon the zealot
Judas Iscariot

U	A	R	E	P	P	J	T	H	A	D	D	A	E	U	S	P
B	Z	F	E	B	I	A	L	V	U	W	B	D	Z	L	B	H
Y	R	E	N	S	L	M	Y	V	H	R	W	Z	L	J	V	I
S	I	M	O	N	P	E	T	E	R	X	J	C	K	X	T	L
Z	O	M	T	J	S	S	H	J	K	G	W	J	B	T	L	I
J	Y	J	U	D	A	S	I	S	C	A	R	I	O	T	E	P
J	A	M	E	S	S	O	N	O	F	Z	E	B	E	D	E	E
I	U	B	G	X	Y	N	Q	N	P	O	G	M	H	C	Z	P
T	P	D	L	Y	J	O	H	N	J	G	J	S	I	O	G	F
M	B	U	C	R	E	F	G	C	O	U	G	W	F	U	Q	W
R	G	Z	A	A	M	A	T	T	H	E	W	K	V	M	H	D
T	H	O	M	A	S	L	D	M	Q	V	I	L	L	N	H	P
D	Y	F	J	F	Z	P	Z	R	P	W	C	G	Y	R	G	E
S	I	M	O	N	T	H	E	Z	E	A	L	O	T	A	Z	C
E	N	D	E	J	B	A	R	T	H	O	L	O	M	E	W	T
Y	S	M	G	I	V	E	Z	Q	F	C	X	D	A	O	C	Z
Q	W	A	T	M	V	U	K	S	Z	T	D	D	M	V	X	Q
H	D	M	D	U	U	S	B	I	O	T	A	N	D	R	E	W

Jesus taught people about God and healed the sick, the blind, deaf, and lame. Everywhere He went, crowds followed.

What did Jesus say His mission here on earth was?
Use the code to find out.

___ ___ ___ ___ ___ ___ ___ ___ ___ ___ ___
13 12 18   15 23 25   23 16   2 26 25

___ ___ ___ ___ ___ ___ ___ ___ ___ ___
20 10 20   25 23 13   22 23 2 18

___ ___ ___ ___ ___ ___ ___ ___ ___ ___ ,
13 23   24 18   15 18 17 9 18 20

___ ___ ___ ___ ___ ___ ___ ___ ___ ___ ,
24 11 13   13 23   15 18 17 9 18

___ ___ ___ ___ ___ ___ ___ ___ ___
26 25 20   13 23   14 10 9 18

___ ___ ___ ___ ___ ___ ___ ___ ___
12 10 15   4 10 16 18 26 15

___ ___ ___ ___ ___ ___ ___
26 17 26 25 15 23 2

___ ___ ___ ___ ___ ___ ___. Matthew 20:28
16 23 17   2 26 25 3

A/26	B/24	C/22	D/20	E/18	F/16	G/14
H/12	I/10	J/8	K/6	L/4	M/2	N/25
O/23	P/21	Q/19	R/17	S/15	T/13	U/11
V/9	W/7	X/5	Y/3	Z/1		

The religious leaders of the day hated Him.
Instead of endorsing the rigorous Jewish laws,
Jesus preached a message of love and forgiveness.

What did Jesus say? Write the letter that comes AFTER the letter under each line to find out.

$\underline{}\ \underline{}\ \underline{}\ \underline{}\ \ \underline{}\ \underline{}\ \underline{}\ \underline{}$
K N U D   X N T Q

$\underline{}\ \underline{}\ \underline{}\ \underline{}\ \underline{}\ \underline{}\ \underline{}\ \ \text{A}\ \underline{}\ \underline{}$
D M D L H D R   M C

$\underline{}\ \underline{}\ \text{A}\ \underline{}\ \underline{}\ \underline{}\ \underline{}\ \underline{}\ \underline{}\ \underline{}\ \underline{}\ \underline{}$
O Q   X E N Q S G N R D

$\underline{}\ \underline{}\ \underline{}\ \underline{}\ \underline{}\ \underline{}\ \underline{}\ \underline{}\ \underline{}\ \underline{}\ \underline{}\ \underline{}$
V G N O D Q R D B T S D

$\underline{}\ \underline{}\ \underline{}.\ \ \underline{}\ \text{A}\ \underline{}\ \underline{}\ \underline{}\ \underline{}\ \underline{}\ 5:44$
X N T   L   S S G D V

A B C D E F G H I J K L M N O P Q R S T U V W X Y Z

However, there was one religious leader, a Pharisee named Nicodemus, who came to see Jesus under cover of darkness. Nicodemus knew that no one could do the miracles Jesus did unless He came from God.

Find the path from Nicodemus to Jesus.

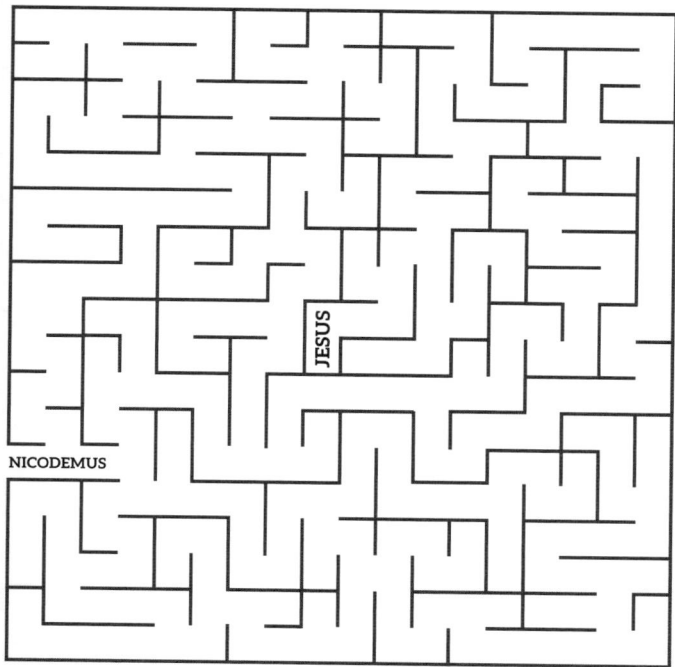

Jesus told Nicodemus no one can see the kingdom of God unless they are born again. Nicodemus did not understand what that meant, so Jesus explained it to him. Jesus told him about eternal life. What did He say?

Cross out words that name a color, number, or animal. Then write the words you have left to read the Bible verse.

sheep	green	may
four	be	brown
The	seven	have
orange	lifted	horse
Son	zebra	eternal
of	up	twenty
Man	that	bear
purple	everyone	life
must	yellow	in
donkey	who	six
black	one	him
eight	believes	red

_____

_____

_____ John 3:14–15

Jesus said God had sent Him to offer salvation to the world. The problem was, and still is today, that people wanted to keep sinning instead of letting God's light of truth shine in their lives. What does the Bible say?

Follow the lines from the letters to the blanks they touch. Write the letters to read the Bible verse.

Whoever lives by

_ _ _ _ _ _ _

_ _ _ _ _

_ _ _ _ _ _ _.

John 3:21

e t h h r t i
o e n m o t
t e c h l h g i t
u s

23

As time went by, the religious leaders plotted to get rid of Jesus once and for all. Why did they want to kill Jesus?

Use the animal code on the next page to find out.

They thought ___ ___ ___ ___ ___ ___ ___ ___ ___

___ ___ ___ ___ ___ ___ ___ ___ ___ ___ ___

in ___ ___ ___, and ___ ___ ___ ___ ___

the ___ ___ ___ ___ ___ ___ ___ ___ ___ ___

___ ___ ___ ___ ___ and ___ ___ ___ ___ ___ ___ our

___ ___ ___ ___ ___ ___ ___ ___ and our

___ ___ ___ ___ ___ ___ ___

___ ___ ___ ___ ___ ___ ___.

John 11:48

E= 🦊	H= 🐰	O= 🐻	V= 🦤	N= 🐫
K= 🐘	P= 🦍	W= 🦡	S= 🦔	Y= 🦬
R= 🐿️	M= 🐢	L= 🦘	T= 🐆	
B= 🐐	C= 🐎	I= 🐖	A= 🐄	

Jesus was betrayed into the hands of His enemies by someone He trusted.

Who betrayed Jesus?

3H0IPSIDEICSECSIOPFLSEIJLUVDEARS

Beginning with the second letter, write every other letter on the line. Then break the letters into words to read the answer.

_____

How much was the betrayer paid?

Beginning with the first number, write every other number or letter on the line to read the answer.

_____

Then Jesus was judged and found guilty, though He never committed a crime. What does the Bible say?

Go down the first row on the grid. When you come to a shaded box, put that letter on the line below the puzzle. Continue to the end of the puzzle. Then break up the letters into words to read the Bible verse.

A													▨	
B														
E		▨		▨										
F														
G														
H			▨											
I													▨	
K						▨								
L		▨												
N														▨
O					▨	▨				▨				
P									▨		▨			
R	▨									▨				
S	▨													
T				▨										
U	▨							▨		▨				
Y		▨												

_____ Isaiah 53:4

Jesus was subjected to unspeakable cruelty and ultimately sacrificed His life on a cross. In the Bible, the prophet Isaiah foretold what would happen. What did he say?

Use the code to find out.

$\overline{19}\ \overline{22}\ \ \overline{4}\ \overline{26}\ \overline{8}\ \ \ \overline{11}\ \overline{18}\ \overline{22}\ \overline{9}\ \overline{24}\ \overline{22}\ \overline{23}$
HE WAS PIERCED

$\overline{21}\ \overline{12}\ \overline{9}\ \ \overline{12}\ \overline{6}\ \overline{9}$
FOR OUR

$\overline{7}\ \overline{9}\ \overline{26}\ \overline{13}\ \overline{8}\ \overline{20}\ \overline{9}\ \overline{22}\ \overline{8}\ \overline{8}\ \overline{18}\ \overline{12}\ \overline{13}\ \overline{8}$,
TRANSGRESSIONS,

$\overline{19}\ \overline{22}\ \ \overline{4}\ \overline{26}\ \overline{8}\ \ \overline{24}\ \overline{9}\ \overline{6}\ \overline{8}\ \overline{19}\ \overline{22}\ \overline{23}$
HE WAS CRUSHED

$\overline{21}\ \overline{12}\ \overline{9}\ \ \overline{12}\ \overline{6}\ \overline{9}$
FOR OUR

$\overline{18}\ \overline{13}\ \overline{18}\ \overline{10}\ \overline{6}\ \overline{18}\ \overline{7}\ \overline{18}\ \overline{22}\ \overline{8}$.
INIQUITIES.

$\overline{18}\ \overline{8}\ \overline{26}\ \overline{18}\ \overline{26}\ \overline{19}$ 53:5a
ISAIAH 53:5a

A/26   B/25   C/24   D/23   E/22   F/21   G/20

H/19   I/18   J/17   K/16   L/15   M/14   N/13

O/12   P/11   Q/10   R/9   S/8   T/7   U/6

V/5   W/4   X/3   Y/2   Z/1

When Jesus died and was buried in a tomb,
His enemies thought they had won the victory.
A centurion watched as Jesus died. What did he say?

Cross out every B, K, and Q. Then write the letters you have left on the lines to read the answer.

_____Mark 15:39

28

But the story wasn't over. Jesus conquered death and rose from the grave! He took our punishment, so we could be forgiven for our sins.

What does the Bible say? Write the letter that comes BEFORE the letter under each line to find out.

THE PUNISHMENT
U I F   Q V O J T I N F O U

THAT BROUGHT
U I B U   C S P V H I U

US PEACE WAS
V T   Q F B D F   X B T

ON HIM, AND BY
P O   I J N ,   B O E   C Z

HIS WOUNDS WE
I J T   X P V O E T   X F

ARE HEALED.
B S F   I F B M F E .

ISAIAH 53:5b
J T B J B I

A B C D E F G H I J K L M N O P Q R S T U V W X Y Z

The resurrection of Jesus from the grave is what we celebrate at Easter. What did the angel say to the women when they saw the empty tomb?

Write the first letter from the name of each picture on the lines under the puzzle. Do this in number order (1, then 2, then 3, etc.). Then break up the letters into words to read the Bible verse.

_____

_____ Luke 24:6

Jesus died and rose again to give us the greatest gift—the gift of salvation.

What does the Bible say? Use the code to find out.

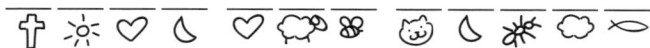

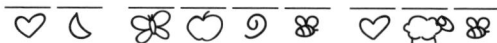

Line 1: ___ ___ ___   ___ ___ ___   ___ ___ ___
Line 2: ___ ___ ___ ___   ___ ___ ___   ___ ___ ___
Line 3: ___ ___ ___ ___   ___ ___ ___   ___ ___ ___ ___ ___
Line 4: ___ ___   ___ ___ ___ ___ ___ ___ ___
Line 5: ___ ___ ___   ___ ___ ___ ___ ___,   ___ ___ ___
Line 6: ___ ___   ___ ___ ___ ___   ___ ___ ___
Line 7: ___ ___ ___ ___ ___.

_ _ _ _ 3:17

Code key:

G = 🌸	D = ⌢	N = ☀	S = 🦋	H = ☁
R = ✳	C = ✌	B = ⭐	A = 🍎	O = ☾
I = ✝	T = ♡	E = 🐝	W = 🐱	J = ∿
L = ☁	M = 🍃	U = ☺	V = ⑨	

Unlike Jesus, every human being has sinned. None of us is perfect. Our sin separates us from God because He is holy and perfect.

Write each word of the Bible verse in the grid. A few letters are given to help you get started.

All have sinned and fall short of the glory of God.
Romans 3:23

We cannot <u>save</u> ourselves. We need a <u>Savior</u>. God <u>loves</u> us so much—even while we are still sinners. He doesn't want even one <u>person</u> to be <u>separated</u> from Him.

The <u>Bible</u> says that "<u>God</u> <u>demonstrates</u> his own love for us in this: <u>While</u> we were still <u>sinners</u>, <u>Christ</u> <u>died</u> for us" (Romans 5:8).

Circle the underlined words hidden in the puzzle.

F	G	A	R	D	G	K	B	L	I	Q	H	J	S
Y	Y	S	U	E	O	P	H	L	T	A	W	U	J
T	X	X	U	M	D	A	M	D	I	E	D	T	V
Z	S	Y	P	O	R	S	V	Z	D	K	E	X	E
P	A	B	C	N	Q	E	C	X	S	M	E	X	N
F	V	P	H	S	Y	D	X	F	I	B	G	B	M
Q	I	E	R	T	W	J	S	K	N	S	R	X	X
C	O	R	I	R	I	R	E	R	N	L	B	V	X
T	R	S	S	A	Q	Y	P	K	E	O	D	W	L
G	A	O	T	T	J	H	A	W	R	V	U	Q	O
M	X	N	U	E	I	E	R	W	S	E	S	I	R
W	S	X	I	S	L	X	A	Z	T	S	A	R	Y
Z	H	U	Z	B	Z	R	T	G	M	U	V	F	L
E	O	I	I	H	D	V	E	E	N	O	E	S	Y
C	Z	B	L	O	W	A	D	P	Q	M	C	V	Q
A	P	W	D	E	D	F	P	W	Z	I	V	O	D

Jesus took our guilt, our shame, and our punishment. He died on the cross for our sins. He died in our place and presents salvation as a gift to us. What does the Bible say?

Use the angle code to write the correct letters on the blanks.

Then read the Bible verse.

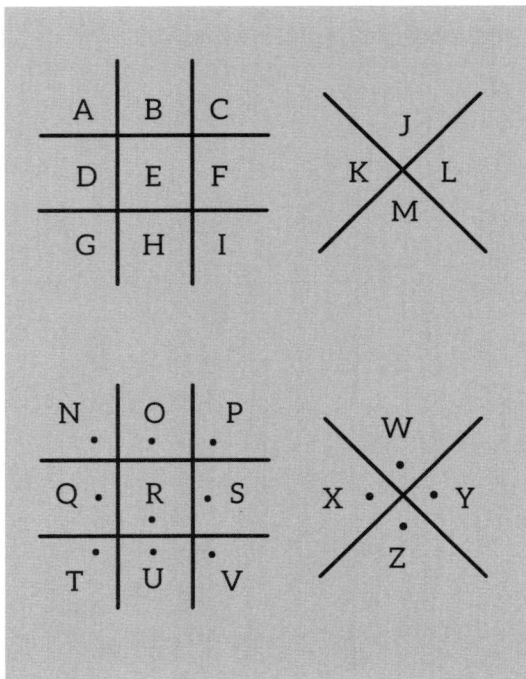

All you have to do to accept this gift is to...

Confess—Tell God you understand you have sinned and own up to the wrongs you have done.

Fill in the blanks with the missing words. Then write them in the grid where they belong. Hint: Look up the verse in your Bible if you need help: 1 John 1:9 (NIV).

If we __ __ __ __ __ __ __ our __ __ __ __,

he is __ __ __ __ __ __ __ __

and __ __ __ __ and will __ __ __ __ __ __ __

us our sins and __ __ __ __ __ __ us from all

__ __ __ __ __ __ __ __ __ __ __ __ __ __ __ __.

1 John 1:9

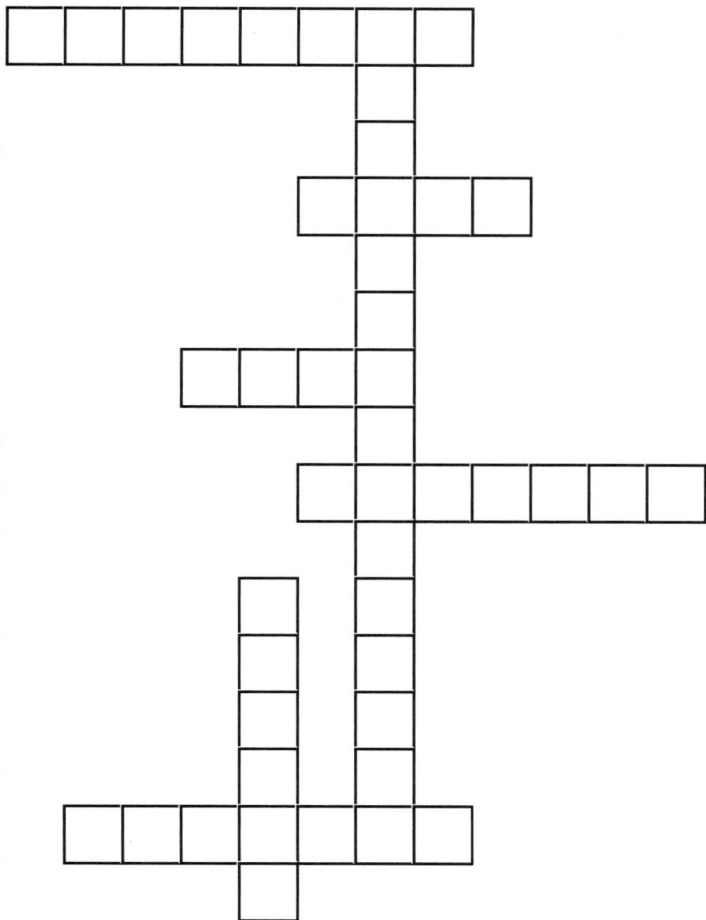

Repent—Tell God you are sorry for what you have done. Express your willingness to leave your sinful life behind and begin a new life with Him.

Cross out words that name a color, vegetable, or animal. Then write the words you have left to read the Bible verse.

orange	gorilla	may
Repent	chipmunk	bean
leopard	green	be
then	so	red
radish	purple	broccoli
and	that	carrot
yellow	corn	wiped
cabbage	your	parrot
pea	green	walrus
turn	sins	out
to	teal	pink
God	monkey	tiger
blue	lion	brown

_____

_____

_____ Acts 3:19

Believe—Jesus died on the cross for your sins, and God has forgiven you.

Go down the first row on the grid. When you come to a shaded box, put that letter on the line below the puzzle. Continue to the end of the puzzle. Then break up the letters into words to read the Bible verse.

A											▧						▧		
B	▧													▧					
D						▧					▧								▧
E	▧		▧	▧		▧			▧						▧		▧		
H				▧															
I		▧		▧									▧						
J							▧												
L	▧						▧						▧	▧					
N			▧							▧									
O				▧					▧										
R				▧															
S							▧	▧								▧			
T			▧																
U						▧				▧									
V		▧															▧		
W									▧										
Y								▧											

_____

_____ Acts 16:31

39

Salvation is a gift that Jesus offers to everyone, but like any gift, we have to decide whether or not to accept it. What does the Bible say?

Use the code to find out.

$\underline{S}\ \underline{A}\ \underline{L}\ \underline{V}\ \underline{A}\ \underline{T}\ \underline{I}\ \underline{O}\ \underline{N}$ is
13 26 25 20 26 2 14 11 4

$\underline{F}\ \underline{O}\ \underline{U}\ \underline{N}\ \underline{D}$ in $\underline{N}\ \underline{O}\ \underline{O}\ \underline{N}\ \underline{E}$
3 11 24 4 12   4 11   11 4 19

$\underline{E}\ \underline{L}\ \underline{S}\ \underline{E}$, for there is no other $\underline{N}\ \underline{A}\ \underline{M}\ \underline{E}$
19 25 13 19   4 26 18 19

under $\underline{H}\ \underline{E}\ \underline{A}\ \underline{V}\ \underline{E}\ \underline{N}$
21 19 26 20 19 4

$\underline{G}\ \underline{I}\ \underline{V}\ \underline{E}\ \underline{N}$ to $\underline{M}\ \underline{A}\ \underline{N}\ \underline{K}\ \underline{I}\ \underline{N}\ \underline{D}$ by
17 14 20 19 4   18 26 4 7 14 4 12

which we must be

$\underline{S}\ \underline{A}\ \underline{V}\ \underline{E}\ \underline{D}$. Acts 4:12
13 26 20 19 12

A/26   B/9   C/6   D/12   E/19   F/3   G/17

H/21   I/14   J/23   K/7   L/25   M/18   N/4

O/11   P/15   Q/22   R/8   S/13   T/2   U/24

V/20   W/5   X/16   Y/10   Z/1

Would you like to experience new life this Easter?
You can receive the gift of salvation right now!
What does the Bible say?

Use the code to find out.

To all who did __ __ __ __ __ __ __   __ __ __ ,

to those who __ __ __ __ __ __ __ __

__ __ __ __ __ __ __ __ __ __ , he gave

the __ __ __ __ __   __ __ __

__ __ __ __ __ __ __ __ __ __ __ __ __ __

__ __ __ __ __ . John 1:12

All you need to do is ask Jesus, and He will forgive you of your sins and enter your life. What does the Bible promise?

Solve the maze. Then write the words you crossed over in order to finish the Bible verse.

_____

_____

_____

_____.

Acts 10:43

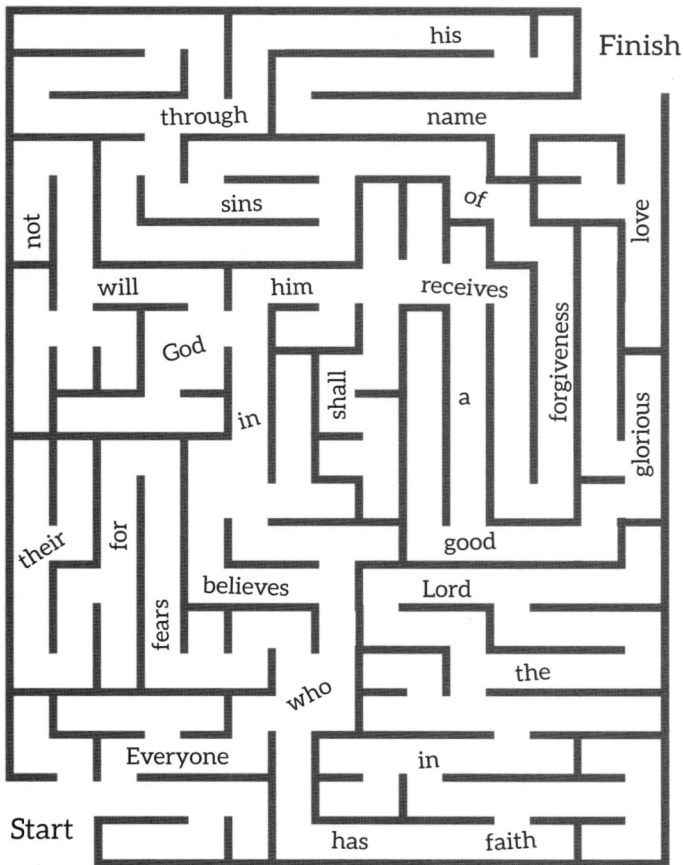

his
through
name
sins
of
love
not
will
him
receives
forgiveness
God
shall
a
glorious
in
their
for
good
fears
believes
Lord
who
the
Everyone
in
Start
has
faith

You can pray the following prayer:

Dear Lord,

Thank You for hearing me and making me aware of my need for a Savior. I know I have sinned and done wrong in Your sight. Forgive me of my sins and give me strength to turn away from them. I want to have a new life with You.

I now confess You are my Lord and Savior. Help me to make You the Master of my life. Guide me in Your ways, so I can learn and grow as Your devoted follower.

Amen

Page 2-3

See, winter, past, rains, over, gone, flowers, earth, season, singing, cooing, doves, heard, land

Page 4

In the hope of eternal life, which God, who does not lie, promised before the beginning of time. Titus 1:2

Page 5

MATTHEW, MARK, LUKE, JOHN / The Four Gospels

Page 6

God saw that it was good. Genesis 1:9

Page 7

Tree of knowledge of good and evil. Genesis 2:17

Page 8

With painful labor Eve would have children. With painful work Adam would grow food for his family. From Genesis 3:16–19

Page 9

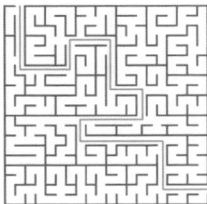

Page 10

The wages of sin is death. Romans 6:23a

Page 11

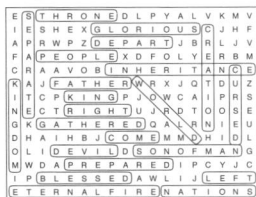

45

Page 12

The gift of God is eternal
life in Christ Jesus our Lord.
Romans 6:23b

Page 13

You, Lord, are forgiving and
good, abounding in love.
Psalm 86:5

Page 14

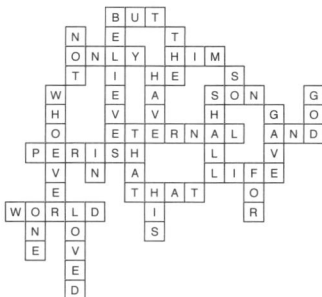

Page 15

The Word became flesh and
made his dwelling among us.
John 1:14

Page 16-17

...tempted in every way, just
as we are—yet he did not sin.
Hebrews 4:15

Page 18

Page 19

The Son of Man did not come
to be served, but to serve, and
to give his life as a ransom for
many. Matthew 20:28

Page 20

Love your enemies and pray
for those who persecute you.
Matthew 5:44

Page 21

Page 22

The Son of Man must be lifted up, that everyone who believes may have eternal life in him. John 3:14–15

Page 23

Whoever lives by the truth comes into the light. John 3:21

Page 24

everyone will believe in him, and then the Romans will come and take away both our temple and our nation. John 11:48

Page 25

HIS DISCIPLE JUDAS
30 PIECES OF SILVER

Page 26

Surely he took up our pain. Isaiah 53:4

Page 27

He was pierced for our transgressions, he was crushed for our iniquities. Isaiah 53:5a

Page 28

Surely this man was the Son of God. Mark 15:39

Page 29

The punishment that brought us peace was on him, and by his wounds we are healed. Isaiah 53:5b

Page 30

He is not here; he has risen! Luke 24:6

Page 31

God did not send his Son into the world to condemn the world, but to save the world. John 3:17

Page 32

Page 33

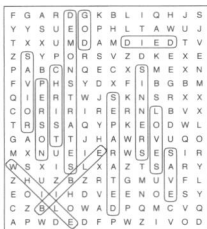

Page 34-35

This is how we know what love is: Jesus Christ laid down his life for us. 1 John 3:16

Page 36-37

confess, sins, faithful, just, forgive, purify, unrighteousness

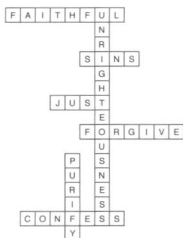

Page 38

Repent, then, and turn to God, so that your sins may be wiped out. Acts 3:19

Page 39

Believe in the Lord Jesus, and you will be saved. Acts 16:31

Page 40

Salvation is found in no one else, for there is no other name under heaven given to mankind by which we must be saved. Acts 4:12

Page 41

To all who did receive him, to those who believed in his name, he gave the right to become children of God. John 1:12

Page 42-43

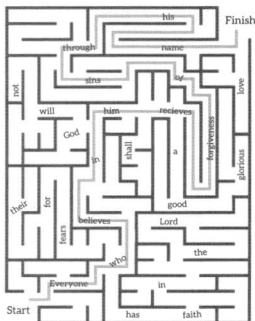